THE COMPLETE

ZURICH TRAVEL GUIDE

2023

Zurich Unveiled: The Ultimate Insider's Travel Guide to Switzerland's Enchanting City"

DENBY DOUGH

Copyright © 2023 by Denby Dough

All rights reserved. No part of this publication may be reproduced, distributed, or transmitted in any form or by any means, including photocopying, recording, or other electronic or mechanical methods, without the prior written permission of the publisher, except in the case of brief quotations embodied in critical reviews and certain other noncommercial uses permitted by copyright law.

Disclaimer: The information provided in this book is for general informational purposes only. While every effort has been made to ensure the accuracy and completeness of the information, the author and publisher assume no responsibility for errors or omissions or any damages resulting from the use of the information contained herein.

Table of Contents

Introduction: Embark on an Unforgettable Journey to Zurich 7

Chapter 1 11

Getting to Zurich: Navigating the Gateway 11

    Flights and Airports that Connect You to Zurich 12

    Tips for Flying to Zurich Without Going Bankrupt 12

    Navigating from the Airport to the City 15

    Zurich by Train: Scenic Trips to the Heart of Switzerland 16

    Driving to Zurich: Routes and Car Rental Tips 17

    Recommended Travel Option 18

Chapter 2 19

Moving Around Zurich: Best Methods of Transport 19

    Tram Tales: Explore Zurich Like a Local 20

    Boats and Bridges: Navigate the Waters of Zurich 21

    Pedestrian Paradises: Foot and Bike Adventures 22

    Recommendations 23

Chapter 3 25

The Culinary Wonders of Zurich: A Taste Sensation 25

    Chocolate Bliss: From Zurich with Love 26

    Cheese, Please! Fondue Frenzy in Zurich 26

    Recommendations 26

Culinary Adventures: Beyond Chocolate and Fondue 29

Recommendations 29

Café Chronicles: Where Coffee Meets Culture 32

Recommendations 33

Zürich by Night 35

Recommendations 37

Chapter 4 39

Hidden Gems and Historical Tales 39

Secrets of the Altstadt: Zurich's Old Town Charms 39

How to Get to the Alstadlt 41

Legends and Lore: Mythical Stories Behind Iconic Landmarks 43

How to get to Lindenhof Hill and the Mühlesteg Bridge 45

How to Get to Niederdorf 47

Chapter 5 49

Lake Zurich: Relaxation, Recreation, and Stunning Views 49

Lakeside Retreats 49

How to Get to the Lake Promenade 51

Lake Cruises: A Voyage into Tranquility 51

Seaside to Mountainside: Outdoor Escapades for Adventurers 53

How to Get to the Mountainside 55

Recommended Modes of Transport for Lake Cruises 56

Chapter 6 59

Contemporary Culture and Creative Quirks 59

    Explore Zurich's Vibrant Contemporary Art Scene 59

    The Hipster's Haven: Trendy Neighborhoods and Local Hangouts 61

    Unique Museums and Eccentric Exhibitions: Prepare to be Mind-Blown! 63

    How to Find Your Way to Zurich's Museums and Art Neighborhoods 65

Chapter 7 67

Retail Therapy: Shopping Extravaganza 67

    Boutique Bliss: Fashion Forward Shopping Districts 67

    Vintage Vista: Discover Retro Treasures in Flea Markets and Thrift Stores 69

    Vintage Boutiques and Consignment Stores 70

    Swiss Souvenirs: Locally Crafted Keepsakes to Bring Home 70

    How to Move Around While Shopping in Zurich 71

Chapter 8 75

Adventure Awaits: Day Trips from Zurich 75

    Alpine Escapades: Skiing, Hiking, and Nature's Marvels 75

    Castles and Countryside: Medieval Marvels Beyond the City 76

    Wine Tasting and Vineyard Hopping: Discover Swiss Vintages 77

    How to Find Your Way Around 79

Best Means of Transport for Day Trips 81

Chapter 9 83

From Festivals to Fond Farewells: Experiencing Zurich's Events 83

Christmas Markets 88

Chapter 10 89

Insider Tips: Making the Most of Your Zurich Adventure 89

Language and Cultural Etiquette: Embrace the Swiss Way of Life 89

Weather Wonders: Dress for the Seasons and Climate 90

Money Matters: Currency, Tipping, and Budgeting Advice 92

Conclusion 95

Forever Enamored: Leaving Zurich with Memories That Last 95

Bon Voyage! Maps and Helpful Resources for Your Zurich Adventure
.... 97

Maps and Navigation 97

Helpful Resources 98

Introduction: Embark on an Unforgettable Journey to Zurich

Welcome, fellow wanderer and travel enthusiast, to the exhilarating world of Zurich! Get ready to embark on an adventure like no other, where vibrant culture, breathtaking landscapes, and Swiss chocolate-induced bliss await you at every turn.

Buckle up because we're about to take off on a journey that will tickle your taste buds, ignite your wanderlust, and leave you yearning for more. I assume you're a first-time Zurich visitor. Even if you aren't, I'm sure you'll find a lot of handy tips and tricks for having the best visit in this guide.

Now, let me help you picture a bit of what you're about to enjoy. Close your eyes and imagine you're strolling through the charming streets of Zurich, surrounded by centuries-old buildings, their facades whispering tales of the city's rich history.

As you meander through the narrow alleys of the Altstadt, you stumble upon hidden gems that even the locals don't know about. And let's not forget the Swiss cuisine, the stuff of foodie dreams!

The city of Zurich is the best place to indulge in a delightful feast of heavenly chocolates that melt in your mouth like a love letter from the cocoa gods. And who can resist dipping morsels of bread into a pot of gooey, molten cheese fondue?

Now, let's talk coffee, my caffeinated comrade. Zurich is a haven where coffee meets culture, where hipster cafes and cozy nooks invite you to sip on a steaming cup of joe while pondering life's mysteries.

Even if you were never a coffee fan, something here will captivate you and ignite your curiosity. You may only start with a taste, but who knows, you may even fall in love with the coffee in Zurich.

And if you're a coffee enthusiast, welcome to one of the world's best coffee havens! As you immerse yourself in the café culture, you'll witness the blend of tradition and innovation where baristas craft intricate latte art.

But wait, there's more to Zurich than just its culinary prowess. Imagine yourself cruising along the sparkling waters of Lake Zurich, surrounded by majestic mountains and emerald-green landscapes. It's a nature lover's paradise where relaxation and recreation go hand in hand.

Dive into the crystal-clear waters, embark on a serene boat ride, or unleash your inner adventurer with thrilling outdoor escapades. Whatever your heart desires, Lake Zurich has it all.

As you glide through the chapters of this lively travel companion, I'll unveil some of the city's hidden treasures and share intriguing historical tales and insider tips to make your Zurich adventure truly unforgettable.

So, fasten your seatbelt, keep your hands and feet inside the guide at all times, and get ready to be swept away into a world of charm, beauty, and laughter. Your journey awaits, and trust me; it's going to be one for the books!

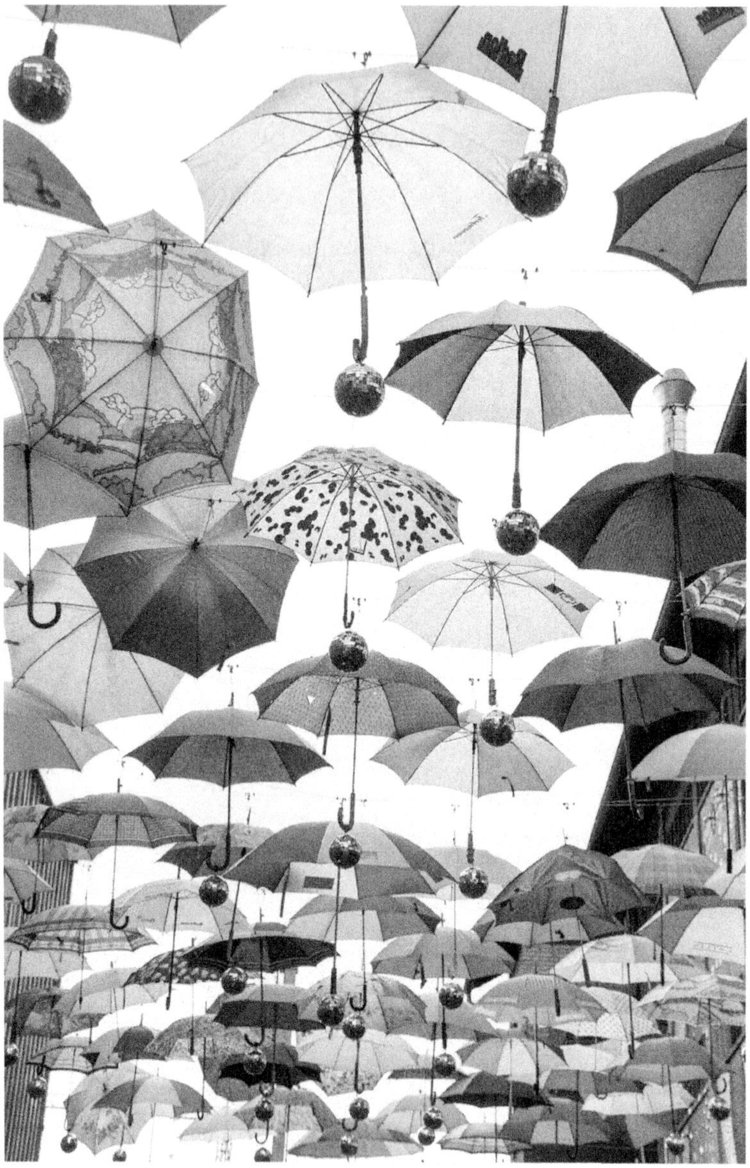

Chapter 1

Getting to Zurich: Navigating the Gateway

Welcome, dear adventurer. Before we delve into all the thrilling experiences awaiting you in Zurich, let's talk about getting there. Yeah, you probably have that sorted, but you can still find a tip or two here to help, or you may find some info even to make you have a change of plans. And if you don't already have your mode of transport chosen, then you're in luck.

In this chapter, we'll dive into the various ways to reach Zurich and navigate the gateway to this captivating city. Whether you're arriving by air, hopping on a train, or embarking on a road trip, I've got you covered. So, fasten your seatbelts and get ready for a smooth journey to the heart of Switzerland!

Flights and Airports that Connect You to Zurich

If you're coming from afar, chances are you'll be landing at one of the airports serving Zurich. The main airport is Zurich Airport (ZRH), conveniently located just 13 kilometers from the city center. With its wide range of international flights, ZRH is a hub for travelers from around the world.

Other nearby airports, like EuroAirport Basel-Mulhouse-Freiburg and Geneva Airport, also offer connections to Zurich. These airports are well-connected to Zurich by train and are great options if you plan to explore more of Switzerland before reaching the city.

Tips for Flying to Zurich Without Going Bankrupt

Oh, the excitement of embarking on a journey to Zurich! But let's face it, getting there without breaking the bank can sometimes feel like a mission impossible.

Well, I have some witty travel tricks up my sleeve to ensure you navigate the gateway without resorting to extreme measures like selling a kidney on the black market. Let's dive in and conquer the skies with finesse!

Budget-Friendly Airlines: Sky-High Savings Without Sacrificing Comfort

Ah, the quest for affordable flights! It's like searching for a unicorn in a sea of leprechauns. But worry not; if you look closely enough, there are budget-friendly airlines that can help you save those precious pennies. Keep an eye out for airlines where comfort meets affordability, and legroom is not just a distant dream.

Timing is Everything: Master the Art of Booking

Timing is everything, my friend! Keep your eye on the digital clock and pounce on those sweet deals during off-peak seasons and random flash sales. And remember, flexibility is your secret weapon.

Be open to playing with your travel dates, and you might just snag a ticket that's cheaper than a pretzel at a street market.

All Hail the Holy Connection: Embrace Layovers like a Travel Ninja

Layovers are like unexpected detours on a road trip. But they can be your ticket to savings and adventure! Embrace the layover like a travel ninja, strategically planning your route to include a pitstop in a vibrant city along the way. Who knows, you might end up exploring the streets of Paris or sampling gelato in Rome before making your way to Zurich. It's like getting two trips for the price of one. Can I get a high-five for layovers?

Luggage Tetris: Maximize Space Like a Packing Magician

Now, let's talk luggage. We've all been there, wrestling with oversized suitcases and trying to squeeze in that extra pair of shoes. Invest your time researching the ways of luggage Tetris.

Roll those clothes, stuff socks into shoes, and make use of every nook and cranny. Conquer the challenge of fitting your entire trip into a suitcase. Plus, you'll have extra room for souvenirs to bring back home!

Navigating from the Airport to the City

Once you land at Zurich Airport, you have several transportation options to reach the city center. The most convenient and time-efficient mode of transport is the train. The airport has its own train station, located beneath the terminal complex.

Trains run frequently and can whisk you to Zurich's main train station, Zurich Hauptbahnhof, in just 10-15 minutes. If you prefer a more personalized experience, taxis and rideshare services are available at the airport.

While this option is more expensive, it offers door-to-door convenience and can be a great choice if you have a lot of luggage or prefer a direct transfer to your accommodation.

Zurich by Train: Scenic Trips to the Heart of Switzerland

Switzerland is renowned for its efficient and picturesque train system, making it a popular mode of transport for travelers. Whether you're arriving from a neighboring city or embarking on a scenic journey through the Swiss Alps, train travel to Zurich is an experience in itself.

If you're coming from within Switzerland, the Swiss Federal Railways (SBB) operates an extensive network of trains connecting Zurich to major cities and towns. The trains are known for their punctuality, comfort, and stunning views along the way. Sit back, relax, and enjoy the picturesque landscapes rolling by your window as you make your way to Zurich.

For an unforgettable adventure, consider taking The Glacier Express or Bernina Express, two iconic train journeys that offer breathtaking views of snow-capped mountains, pristine lakes, and charming alpine villages.

These routes are a feast for the eyes and provide a unique perspective of Switzerland's natural beauty.

Driving to Zurich: Routes and Car Rental Tips

If you prefer the freedom and flexibility of a road trip, driving to Zurich can be an exciting adventure. Switzerland has a well-maintained road infrastructure and stunning landscapes, making it a joy to explore by car.

If you're coming from neighboring countries, such as Germany, France, or Italy, driving to Zurich is a viable option. The road networks are well-developed, and you can enjoy the scenic beauty of the Swiss countryside along the way.

Just remember to familiarize yourself with the local traffic rules and regulations, including speed limits and parking restrictions. Renting a car is a popular choice if you want to explore beyond the city limits and have the flexibility to visit nearby attractions at your own pace.

Zurich has several car rental agencies where you can easily rent a vehicle for your adventure. Be sure to check the requirements, such as age restrictions and driver's license validity, before making a reservation.

Recommended Travel Option

While all three modes of transportation have their advantages, the train is often the most convenient and efficient way to reach Zurich. Switzerland's train network is highly reliable, providing frequent connections to Zurich from various cities and airports.

It offers stunning views and comfortable travel and eliminates the hassle of parking and navigating unfamiliar roads. Additionally, once you're in Zurich, the city's efficient public transportation system can easily take you to your desired destinations.

So, dear adventurous amigo, find your way to Zurich without taking drastic measures. Embark on this journey with wit, charm, and a few tricks up your sleeves. Bon voyage, and may your travel adventures be filled with laughter, savings, and memorable experiences!

Chapter 2

Moving Around Zurich: Best Methods of Transport

Now that you know how you want to get to Zurich, it's time to consider how you'll move around once you're in the city. I included this chapter because I have learned that it's one thing to move around in a city, and it's another thing to actually *enjoy* moving around in a city. I wish for you to have a taste of the latter, so be sure to read through carefully.

This is where we uncover the best methods of transport for navigating the charming city of Zurich. From gliding through the city on trams to exploring the picturesque waters and embracing the pedestrian-friendly culture, Zurich offers a range of transportation options to suit every traveler's preference.

So, let's dive right in and discover the delightful ways to move around Zurich!

Tram Tales: Explore Zurich Like a Local

When it comes to getting around Zurich like a local, there's nothing quite like hopping on a tram. Trams are a vital part of Zurich's public transportation system. They provide frequent services and comprehensive coverage, making it easy to navigate around the city.

They take you through picturesque routes, offering glimpses of Zurich's beautiful landscapes and architectural wonders. Riding the tram allows you to immerse yourself in the local culture and observe the rhythm of daily life in Zurich. Here are some tips for using the tram:

Tram Lines: Zurich boasts an extensive tram network with numerous lines covering the city and its outskirts. Each line has its own unique charm, taking you through vibrant neighborhoods, past historic landmarks, and alongside picturesque parks. Whether you're heading to the trendy Kreis 4 or exploring the historic Altstadt, trams can take you there with ease.

Ticketing: To ride the trams, you'll need a valid ticket.

Tickets can be purchased at ticket machines located at tram stops or through mobile apps. The Zurich Card is a popular option for visitors, offering unlimited travel on public transportation, including trams, buses, and trains, for a specified duration.

I've included information on how to get the card in the last part of this book (Helpful Resources)

Boats and Bridges: Navigate the Waters of Zurich

Zurich's stunning lake and rivers make boat rides an enchanting way to travel and soak up the city's scenic beauty. Here's what you need to know about navigating the waters of Zurich:

Lake Zurich Boat Cruises: Step aboard a boat and embark on a leisurely cruise along Lake Zurich. Admire the panoramic views of the city skyline and the snow-capped Alps in the distance.

Boat cruises often offer narrated tours, providing interesting insights into the city's history and landmarks.

River Limmat: The River Limmat flows through the heart of Zurich, dividing the city into its east and west sides. Explore the city's vibrant riverfront promenades and cross the numerous bridges that connect the neighborhoods. You can even take a river taxi for a unique and scenic way to travel between different parts of the city.

Pedestrian Paradises: Foot and Bike Adventures

Zurich is a pedestrian-friendly city, encouraging exploration on foot and by bike. Lace up your walking shoes or hop on a bicycle to experience the city's charm up close. Here's why exploring on foot and bike is a fantastic way to get around:

Walking: Zurich's compact size and well-designed layout make it an ideal city for walking. While taking a leisurely stroll along the vibrant streets, you'll discover hidden alleyways and neighborhood gems.

You'll come across charming cafes, boutiques, and historic landmarks at every turn. Walking allows you to immerse yourself in the city's atmosphere, interact with locals, and stumble upon unexpected delights.

Biking: If you prefer a more active approach to exploring Zurich, renting a bike is a fantastic option. The city is equipped with an extensive network of bike paths, making it safe and enjoyable to pedal your way around.

Rent a bike from one of the many bike-sharing services, or choose a guided bike tour to discover Zurich's highlights while enjoying the fresh air and scenic routes.

Recommendations

While each mode of transport in Zurich has its advantages, the best method for getting around ultimately depends on your preferences and itinerary. To make the most of your Zurich experience, I recommend a combination of tram rides, boat cruises, and walking or biking.

Start your day by hopping on a tram to reach your desired neighborhood or attraction quickly and efficiently. Enjoy the convenience and comprehensive coverage of the tram network as you explore different parts of the city. For a unique perspective, embark on a boat cruise along Lake Zurich or take a river taxi to experience the city from the water. These scenic rides offer stunning views and a relaxed atmosphere.

Finally, to truly immerse yourself in the charm of Zurich, set aside time for leisurely walks and bike rides. Wander through the narrow streets of the Altstadt, discover hidden squares, and soak up the city's vibrant energy. Renting a bike allows you to venture a bit further and explore the city's outskirts or cycle along the picturesque River Limmat.

By combining these modes of transport, you'll have a well-rounded and delightful experience of moving around Zurich, embracing its unique charm from various perspectives.

Remember to plan your journeys in advance, consider the Zurich Card for unlimited travel, and always check the local transportation schedules for any updates or changes.

Chapter 3

The Culinary Wonders of Zurich: A Taste Sensation

Welcome to the tantalizing world of Swiss cuisine, where every bite is a symphony of flavors that will transport you to gastronomic bliss. In this chapter, we'll embark on a mouthwatering journey through the culinary wonders of Zurich, indulging in heavenly chocolates, succulent cheese fondues, and a myriad of other delectable delights.

Prepare to awaken your taste buds and surrender to the irresistible allure of Swiss gastronomy. From the moment you take your first bite, you'll be enchanted by the sheer perfection and attention to detail that goes into each dish.

Whether you're a self-proclaimed chocoholic, a cheese connoisseur, or simply someone who appreciates good food, this chapter is your passport to experiencing the true essence of Swiss gastronomy. Let's delve into the delectable delights that await!

Chocolate Bliss: From Zurich with Love

Let's begin with some sweet, sweet chocolate, shall we? Since you're already here, there's no reason to delay delving into all the heavenly sweetness this city offers. Indulge in the silky, smooth goodness of Swiss chocolate that melts in your mouth like a dream.

Cheese, Please! Fondue Frenzy in Zurich

Cheese lovers, rejoice! It's time to dip, dunk, and devour the irresistible Swiss cheese fondue. Grab your friends or make new ones as you gather around a bubbling cauldron of melted cheese goodness.

Recommendations

1. Sprüngli Confiserie

Nestled on the famous Bahnhofstrasse, this place is a chocolate lover's dream come true. Brace yourself for a tantalizing array of exquisite chocolates, from smooth truffles to decadent pralines. But wait, there's more! They are also renowned for their Luxemburgerli macarons, those little bites of heaven that will have you reaching for more.

So, make your way to Bahnhofstrasse, follow the scent of cocoa, and prepare for a chocolate experience that will leave you floating on a cloud of pure bliss.

Bahnhofstrasse 21, 8001 Zurich.   +41 44 224 46

2. Chäsalp

Picture this - a cozy restaurant tucked away in the city, where traditional Swiss cuisine takes center stage, and cheese reigns supreme. Welcome to Chäsalp, my friend. This charming eatery is a cheese enthusiast's haven. And what better way to celebrate the art of cheese than indulging in a bubbling pot of fondue?

Chäsalp serves up a fondue that is sheer perfection - creamy, flavorful, and guaranteed to make you say, "Ooh la la." Imagine dipping a piece of crusty bread into that molten cheese, savoring the rich, gooey goodness that will warm your soul.

Tobelhofstrasse 236, 8044 Zürich.   +41 44 260 75 75

3. Confiserie Honold

Prepare to enter a chocolate wonderland as you step into Confiserie Honold. Located in Rennweg, this chocolate haven is where dreams are made of. As soon as you step inside, you'll be greeted by a display of handmade chocolates that are truly works of art.

From luscious truffles to delicate pralines, each piece is crafted with love and attention to detail. Take a moment to inhale the sweet aroma that fills the air and let your taste buds anticipate the explosion of flavors that await.

Rennweg 53, 8001 Zürich +41 (0)44 211 52 58

PS. Confiserie Honold and Sprüngli Confiserie have multiple locations across the city. Call to confirm the one closest to you. Bon appétit!

Culinary Adventures: Beyond Chocolate and Fondue

Not just chocolate and cheeses, Zurich's culinary scene is a vibrant tapestry of flavors from around the world. From Michelin-starred restaurants to cozy little eateries tucked away in hidden corners, there's something to satiate every craving. Don't miss out on trying traditional Swiss dishes like Zürcher Geschnetzeltes (sliced veal in a creamy sauce) or Rösti (crispy potato pancakes) that will leave you licking your lips and asking for seconds.

So, don't limit yourself to chocolate and fondue alone. Explore, savor, and let your taste buds embark on a culinary adventure that will leave you with memories as delicious as the dishes themselves. Bon appétit!

Recommendations

1. Try Zürcher Geschnetzeltes at Zeughauskeller

For a taste of traditional Swiss cuisine, indulge in Zürcher Geschnetzeltes, sliced veal in a creamy sauce.

Head to Zeughauskeller, a historic restaurant known for its hearty Swiss dishes, including their famous Zürcher Geschnetzeltes. The tender veal and rich sauce will leave you wanting more.

Bahnhofstrasse 28a, 8001 Zurich   +41442201515

2. Try Rösti, at Swiss Chuchi

To experience the crispy delight of Rösti, visit Swiss Chuchi, a charming restaurant dedicated to Swiss cuisine. Their Rösti is a standout, perfectly golden and crispy on the outside and soft on the inside. Pair it with a delicious selection of toppings, such as cheese, bacon, or fried eggs, for a satisfying meal.

Rosengasse 10, 8001 Zürich   +41 44 266 96 66

3. Try Sushi at Tao's

If you're in the mood for sushi, make your way to Tao's, a popular Japanese restaurant with a contemporary atmosphere. Their skilled chefs create sushi masterpieces using fresh and high-quality ingredients. From classic rolls to creative specialties, Tao's will satisfy your sushi cravings.

Augustinergasse 3, 8001 Zurich   +41 44 448 11 22

4. Mediterannean Delights at Maison Manese

Indulge in Mediterranean flavors at Maison Manesse, a trendy restaurant that combines Swiss and Mediterranean influences. Explore their innovative menu featuring dishes like grilled octopus, homemade pasta, and flavorful mezze platters. Maison Manesse offers a delightful fusion of cuisines that will transport your taste buds to the Mediterranean coast.

Hopfenstrasse 2, 8045 Zurich   +41444620101

5. Indian Cuisine at Hiltl

For a flavorful Indian feast, head to Hiltl), the world's oldest vegetarian restaurant that also offers an extensive selection of Indian dishes. Delight in aromatic curries, flavorful biryanis, and mouthwatering vegetarian specialties that showcase the diverse flavors of India.

Sihlstrasse 28, 8001 Zurich   +41442277000

Café Chronicles: Where Coffee Meets Culture

As a self-proclaimed coffee enthusiast, let me tell you, Zurich knows how to brew a mean cup of joe.

Prepare to be amazed by the baristas of Zurich who transform coffee into a work of art. Be it delicate latte art or the precision of a perfectly brewed espresso, these coffee virtuosos take their craft seriously.

Don't be surprised if you find yourself staring at your cup in awe, contemplating whether to drink it or frame it.

In Zurich, you'll find cafés that offer more than just a great cup of coffee; they come with jaw-dropping views as well. Imagine sipping your espresso while gazing at the shimmering waters of Lake Zurich or enjoying a latte overlooking the iconic Grossmünster. These cafés offer the perfect blend of caffeine and stunning vistas, creating an experience you won't soon forget.

Recommendations

1. Café Odeon

This one's a café with a touch of history and a whole lot of elegance. The ambiance is simply divine, with its vintage decor and cozy seating areas. About coffee, they take their craft seriously here. You can expect a perfectly brewed cup of java that will awaken your senses with its rich aroma and smoothness; it's like a warm hug for your taste buds. Don't even get me started on their pastries. They're a work of art!

Limmatquai 2, 8001 Zurich   +41442511650

2. Milchbar

Milchbar is perfect if you're in the mood for a hip and trendy café that knows how to make coffee right. The spot is tucked away on Kappelergasse, so it's sort of a hidden gem. The vibe here is laid-back and effortlessly cool, with funky decor and a friendly atmosphere.

Talking about the coffee - they serve artisanal coffee that will blow your mind.

The baristas here are like coffee wizards; brewing up some of the best cups of joe you'll ever taste. And the pastries? Oh boy, they're divine. From flaky croissants to mouthwatering cakes, every bite is a little piece of heaven.

Kappelergasse 16, 8001 Zürich   +41(0)44 211 9012

3. Grande Café

If you're in the mood for a coffee spot that's buzzing with energy and has a vibrant atmosphere, try Grande Café. The place is always busy since it's a favorite among locals and tourists alike. As soon as you step inside, you'll be greeted by the lively chatter and the smell of freshly brewed coffee. The coffee is top-notch, the vibe is electric, and it's the perfect spot for people-watching and soaking up the local scene.

Limmatquai 118, 8001 Zürich   +41442621516

Zürich by Night

When the sun sets, and the moon takes center stage, Zurich reveals its vibrant nightlife and gastronomic wonders. Get ready to embark on a nocturnal gastronomic adventure like no other!

Gourmet Night Markets

Step into the magical world of Zurich's night markets, where tantalizing aromas fill the air and food stalls beckon with irresistible treats. Explore the trendy Street Food Festival, where you can feast on a global culinary journey, from mouthwatering burgers to exotic street eats. PS. Come with an empty stomach and a sense of culinary adventure!

Wine and Dine: Top Eateries for Night Owls

For those seeking a refined dining experience, Zurich boasts an array of elegant restaurants that come alive after dark. Immerse yourself in a world of exquisite flavors, where expertly crafted dishes are paired with the finest wines.

Indulge in a romantic candlelit dinner or gather your friends for a gastronomic feast that will leave you with unforgettable memories and satisfied taste buds.

Bars and Brews:

Zurich's nightlife scene offers a diverse range of bars and breweries that cater to every palate. From chic cocktail lounges to lively beer gardens, there's a spot for everyone to raise a glass and toast to the night. Sip on expertly crafted cocktails, sample local craft beers, or dare to try the legendary absinthe, all while immersing yourself in the vibrant energy of Zurich after hours.

Late-Night Dessert Delights

Who says the fun ends with the main course? In Zurich, a dessert is an art form that deserves its own spotlight. Indulge your sweet tooth with delectable pastries, heavenly ice creams, or a heavenly slice of Swiss chocolate cake. Whether you have a penchant for delicate macarons or crave the comforting warmth of a freshly baked Swiss apple strudel, Zurich's dessert scene will satisfy even the most discerning sweet tooth.

Recommendations

1. Street Food Festival

For a vibrant culinary experience, keep an eye out for the Street Food Festival, a lively night market that showcases a diverse selection of global street food. The festival pops up in various locations throughout Zurich, so check their website or social media for upcoming events. It's a fantastic opportunity to indulge in a wide range of international flavors.

www.streetfoodfest.ch/

2. Frau Gerolds Garten

A trendy open-air venue with food trucks, bars, and a vibrant atmosphere, offering a variety of culinary delights. Geroldstrasse 23/23a, 8005 Zurich   +41789716764

3. Jules Verne Panorama Bar

A rooftop bar with panoramic views of Zurich, offering a wide range of cocktails and a chic ambiance.

Uraniastrasse 9, 8001 Zürich   +41438886667

These are just a few suggestions to kick-start your culinary adventures in Zurich, my friend. From traditional Swiss dishes to international delights, the city's food scene has something to please every palate. Bon appétit!

PS. Remember to check the opening hours and make reservations where necessary, as these popular places tend to fill up quickly. Enjoy your culinary exploration of Zurich's finest establishments and have a memorable gastronomic journey!

Chapter 4

Hidden Gems and Historical Tales

Welcome to another exciting aspect of Zurich that I'm about to take you through. In this chapter, we'll dive into the enchanting world of hidden gems and historical tales that lie within the city's charming streets. Get ready to unveil Altstadt's secrets and discover the mythical stories behind iconic landmarks. Get your walking shoes, grab a cup of Swiss hot chocolate, and let's explore!

Secrets of the Altstadt: Zurich's Old Town Charms

Welcome to the captivating world of Zurich's Altstadt, where history comes alive and hidden secrets await your discovery. In this section, we will peel back the layers of time and unveil the charming mysteries that lie within the cobblestone streets and quaint squares.

Immerse yourself in the whimsical stories of the Altstadt and uncover the hidden gems that make this historic district truly enchanting.

The Curious Case of the Mysterious Fountain

As you wander through Zurich's Altstadt, you'll stumble upon an intriguing sight—a fountain adorned with an assortment of whimsical figures. But did you know that this fountain, known as the Zürcher Kindl Brunnen, has a secret hidden within its waters?

Legend has it that if you make a wish and toss a coin into the fountain, the Zürcher Kindl (a child-like figure) will grant your wish with a mischievous twist. One traveler, eager for a sunny day, wished for clear skies, only to find herself caught in a sudden downpour moments later!

So, be careful what you wish for, and keep an eye out for that playful Zürcher Kindl.

Schipfe: The Alley of Secrets and Surprises

Nestled within Altstadt's labyrinth of narrow streets lies the charming Schipfe Alley.

This seemingly ordinary alley holds a delightful secret. Follow the cobbled path, and you'll discover hidden doorways leading to quirky artisan workshops, cozy cafés, and antique stores brimming with treasures from centuries past.

Rumor has it that Schipfe Alley was once a meeting place for local artists and thinkers, who would gather here to share their creative musings. Perhaps the artistic energy still lingers in the air, inspiring the alley's present-day inhabitants.

How to Get to the Alstadlt

To reach Altstadt, the historic heart of Zurich, you'll find a variety of convenient transportation options. One of the best ways to immerse yourself in the atmosphere of the Old Town is by walking. Lace up your comfortable shoes, and meander through the narrow streets at your own pace.

Walking allows you to appreciate the intricate details of the architecture and stumble upon hidden gems along the way. Best of all, it's free!

If you're staying farther away or prefer a faster mode of transport, Zurich's efficient public transportation network is at your service. Trams and buses crisscross the city, and you can easily find connections to the Altstadt.

A single tram or bus ticket typically costs around CHF 2.80 to CHF 4.40, depending on the duration of your journey. You can purchase tickets from vending machines at tram stops or through the SBB Mobile app.

My Recommendation

While public transportation is efficient and suitable for longer distances, I highly recommend taking a leisurely stroll through the Altstadt to fully appreciate its charms and hidden corners.

Legends and Lore: Mythical Stories Behind Iconic Landmarks

Prepare to be transported into a realm of legends and folklore as we delve into the mythical tales that shroud Zurich's iconic landmarks.

In this section, we will unlock the secrets of Lindenhof Hill, where a dragon guards a hidden treasure, and wander the Mühlesteg Bridge, adorned with love locks that hold the power of eternal love.

The Dragon's Treasure at Lindenhof Hill

Perched high above the Limmat River, Lindenhof Hill offers not only breathtaking views but also a tale of mystery and wonder. Legend has it that beneath the hill lies a hidden cave where a mighty dragon guards a priceless treasure.

Many adventurers have tried to uncover the dragon's secret hoard, but all have returned empty-handed—some with only charred pants to tell the tale.

So, as you stroll through Lindenhof Hill, keep an eye out for any signs of fire-breathing reptiles, and beware of wearing anything too flammable.

The Love Locks of Mühlesteg Bridge

Romantics and dreamers alike flock to the picturesque Mühlesteg Bridge, not only for its stunning views but also for a heartwarming tradition. Couples from around the world come here to proclaim their love by attaching a padlock to the bridge's railings and throwing the key into the Limmat River.

Legend has it that these love locks hold the power to bind two souls together forever. Some locals claim that the bridge has become so laden with locks that it occasionally flirts with the danger of collapsing under the weight of all that love. Whether you believe in the magical properties of love locks or not, it's a heartwarming sight to behold.

How to get to Lindenhof Hill and the Mühlesteg Bridge

Lindenhof Hill and the Mühlesteg Bridge, our mythical landmarks, are conveniently located within the Altstadt, making them easily accessible on foot.

If you're feeling adventurous and up for a bit of exercise, you can also rent a bicycle. Zurich has an extensive network of bike lanes and rental stations, with prices starting at around CHF 6 per hour. Pedaling your way to Lindenhof Hill and the Mühlesteg Bridge adds a fun and active twist to your exploration.

Surprising Side Streets: Unexpected Gems Off the Beaten Path

In this section, I'll take you on a journey through the charming neighborhood of Niederdorf, where every street corner reveals a delightful surprise and lead you to the tantalizing Flavour Alley, a haven for food enthusiasts seeking unique culinary experiences.

Get ready to explore the unexpected and embrace the joy of discovering Zurich's hidden gems nestled in the city's vibrant side streets.

The Quirky Charm of Niederdorf

As you stroll through the colorful streets of Niederdorf, you'll encounter an array of eclectic shops, trendy boutiques, and lively bars. But there's one particular street that stands out from the rest—Niederdorfstrasse, known affectionately as "Niederdorf's Quirky Lane."

This narrow and winding street is a treasure trove of eccentricity. You'll find shops selling vintage vinyl records, quirky handmade crafts, and even a store dedicated solely to rubber ducks of all shapes and sizes. It's the perfect place to unleash your inner whimsy and indulge in a little retail therapy with a twist.

The Alley of Culinary Surprises

Tucked away in a quiet corner of Zurich's old town lies a narrow alleyway that will tickle your taste buds and ignite your culinary senses. Welcome to "Flavour Alley."

This hidden gem is home to a collection of tiny, hole-in-the-wall eateries serving up delectable delights from around the world. From mouthwatering Mexican tacos to fragrant Indian curries and from traditional Swiss fondue to tantalizing Thai street food, Flavour Alley is a food lover's paradise.

But here's the catch—there are no menus to be found. Instead, the friendly owners will surprise you with their daily specials, ensuring that each visit to Flavour Alley is a unique and delicious adventure.

How to Get to Niederdorf

Niederdorf, our vibrant neighborhood of unexpected treasures, is also conveniently located within the Altstadt, making it easily accessible on foot. To reach Flavour Alley, which is tucked away in a quiet corner of the Altstadt, you can once again rely on walking.

So, go forth and uncover Zurich's hidden charms with a sense of curiosity and a touch of whimsy. May you find laughter in the legends, joy in the discoveries, and unforgettable memories in every hidden nook and cranny. Happy exploring!

48 | **The Complete Zurich Travel Guide 2023**

Chapter 5

Lake Zurich: Relaxation, Recreation, and Stunning Views

In this chapter, we will explore the captivating beauty of Lake Zurich, from its tranquil shores to the mesmerizing vistas that surround it. So, pack your swimsuit, bring your sense of adventure, and let's dive into the serenade of nature at Lake Zurich.

Lakeside Retreats

Picture yourself lounging on a sun-kissed lakeside terrace, sipping a refreshing drink while gazing at the glimmering waters of Lake Zurich. Along the shores, you'll find a multitude of tranquil spots to relax and soak up the serenity.

Strandbad Tiefenbrunnen.

One popular lakeside retreat is the enchanting Strandbad Tiefenbrunnen.

With its sandy beach, crystal-clear waters, and lush greenery, it offers the perfect setting for a leisurely swim or a sunbathing session. If you prefer a more secluded experience, head to one of the quieter hidden coves along the lake, where you can find your own private slice of lakeside bliss.

The Lake Promenade

Take a leisurely stroll along the Lake Promenade, a picturesque pathway that meanders along the water's edge. As you wander, you'll be treated to breathtaking views of the lake, framed by the majestic Swiss Alps in the distance.

The Lake Promenade is not only a feast for the eyes but also a hub of activity. You'll encounter joggers, cyclists, and families enjoying picnics on the grassy knolls. So, grab a gelato from one of the nearby vendors, take a seat on a park bench, and let the soothing ambiance of Lake Zurich wash over you.

How to Get to the Lake Promenade

To reach the lakeside retreats and the Lake Promenade, you have several convenient transportation options. The most recommended mode of transport is walking, as it allows you to fully immerse yourself in the lakeside ambiance and take in the stunning views along the way. Plus, walking is free and gives you the freedom to explore at your own pace.

If you're staying farther away or prefer a quicker option, public transportation is readily available. Trams and buses in Zurich connect you to various points along the lake, and a single ticket typically costs around CHF 2.80 to CHF 4.40, depending on the duration of your journey. Public transportation offers convenience and saves time, especially if you're limited in time or have a longer distance to cover.

Lake Cruises: A Voyage into Tranquility

Step aboard and let the gentle sway of the boat carry you into a world of tranquility. In this section, we embark on a soothing voyage through the crystal waters of Lake Zurich.

Whether you choose a leisurely boat tour or a romantic moonlit cruise, prepare to be captivated by panoramic vistas, the gentle lapping of the waves, and the serenade of nature. Relax, rejuvenate, and let the peacefulness of the lake envelop your senses.

Lake Zurich Boat Tours

Step aboard a boat and immerse yourself in the tranquility of Lake Zurich. Boat tours offer a unique perspective, allowing you to witness the serene beauty of the lake from the middle of its crystal-clear waters.

Cruise along the shoreline, passing charming villages, luxurious mansions, and verdant landscapes. The gentle lapping of the waves against the boat, combined with the panoramic views, creates a symphony of serenity that will rejuvenate your senses.

Romantic Moonlit Cruises

As dusk settles over Lake Zurich, a romantic ambiance fills the air. It's the perfect time to embark on a moonlit cruise, where the shimmering moonlight dances on the water's surface, casting a magical glow.

Savor a candlelit dinner aboard a cruise ship, accompanied by live music and breathtaking vistas. Let the gentle sway of the boat and the moon's enchanting embrace create an unforgettable experience that will ignite the sparks of romance.

Whether you're celebrating a special occasion or simply indulging in a moment of bliss, a moonlit cruise on Lake Zurich is an experience that will leave a lasting impression.

Seaside to Mountainside: Outdoor Escapades for Adventurers

Calling all adventurers! In this section, we venture from the lakeside to the mountainside, exploring the thrilling outdoor escapades that await at Lake Zurich. Lace up your hiking boots, grab your mountain bike, and get ready to embrace the exhilaration of nature's playground. With hiking trails that unveil breathtaking views and mountain biking routes that offer adrenaline-pumping descents, Lake Zurich invites you to embark on unforgettable outdoor adventures amidst the majestic Swiss Alps.

Seaside Thrills: Watersports and More

Lake Zurich isn't just for relaxation; it's a playground for outdoor enthusiasts. Dive into the crystal-clear waters and immerse yourself in a world of watersports and thrilling activities.

For the adrenaline seekers, try your hand at wakeboarding or water skiing. Enjoy the rush as you glide across the lake. If you prefer a more leisurely adventure, grab a paddle and hop on a stand-up paddleboard (SUP).

If you're looking to explore beneath the surface, why not try scuba diving or snorkeling in Lake Zurich? Discover a hidden world teeming with vibrant aquatic life and explore submerged treasures beneath the tranquil surface.

Mountainside Escapades: Hiking and Biking

While the lake offers its own charm, it is also a gateway to the stunning Swiss Alps. Choose from an array of hiking trails that cater to all skill levels, from leisurely lakeside strolls to challenging mountain treks.

Breathe in the fresh alpine air as you traverse lush forests, meadows adorned with wildflowers, and panoramic viewpoints that showcase the grandeur of the surrounding peaks.

Mountain biking enthusiasts will find plenty of exhilarating trails to explore, with varying levels of difficulty. Feel the thrill of descending winding paths, navigating rocky terrains, and experiencing the sheer joy of speed and freedom in the midst of nature's playground.

How to Get to the Mountainside

To reach the mountainside and hiking trails surrounding Lake Zurich, you can take advantage of public transportation or choose private transportation options such as taxis or rental cars.

Public transportation, such as trams and buses, can take you to various starting points for hiking or biking adventures. The cost of public transportation for longer journeys may range from CHF 2.80 to CHF 4.40 for a single ticket.

If you prefer the flexibility of private transportation, renting a car allows you to reach specific trailheads and access more remote areas. Rental car prices vary depending on the duration of the rental and the type of vehicle, but it is important to consider parking fees and availability, especially in popular areas.

Overall, the recommended mode of transport depends on your preferences, accessibility, and the specific locations you wish to explore.

Recommended Modes of Transport for Lake Cruises

To embark on a boat tour or a moonlit cruise, the starting point is usually the Bürkliplatz, conveniently located near the city center. You can easily reach Bürkliplatz by walking from nearby areas or using public transportation.

Boat tours and cruises on Lake Zurich typically have regular departures and varying durations.

The cost of boat tours ranges from around CHF 10 for shorter trips to CHF 30 or more for longer excursions.

Moonlit cruises with dinner and entertainment are generally priced higher, starting from CHF 80 and up, depending on the package.

Ultimately, both boat tours and moonlit cruises offer their own charm. If you're seeking a more immersive experience and a closer connection with the lake, I recommend a boat tour. However, if you're celebrating a special occasion or looking for a romantic experience, a moonlit cruise with dinner is a wonderful choice.

Remember to consider the advantages of each mode of transport, evaluate your budget, and choose the option that best suits your needs and desired level of exploration.

Embrace the journey, enjoy the serenade of nature, and make unforgettable memories as you explore the wonders of Lake Zurich.

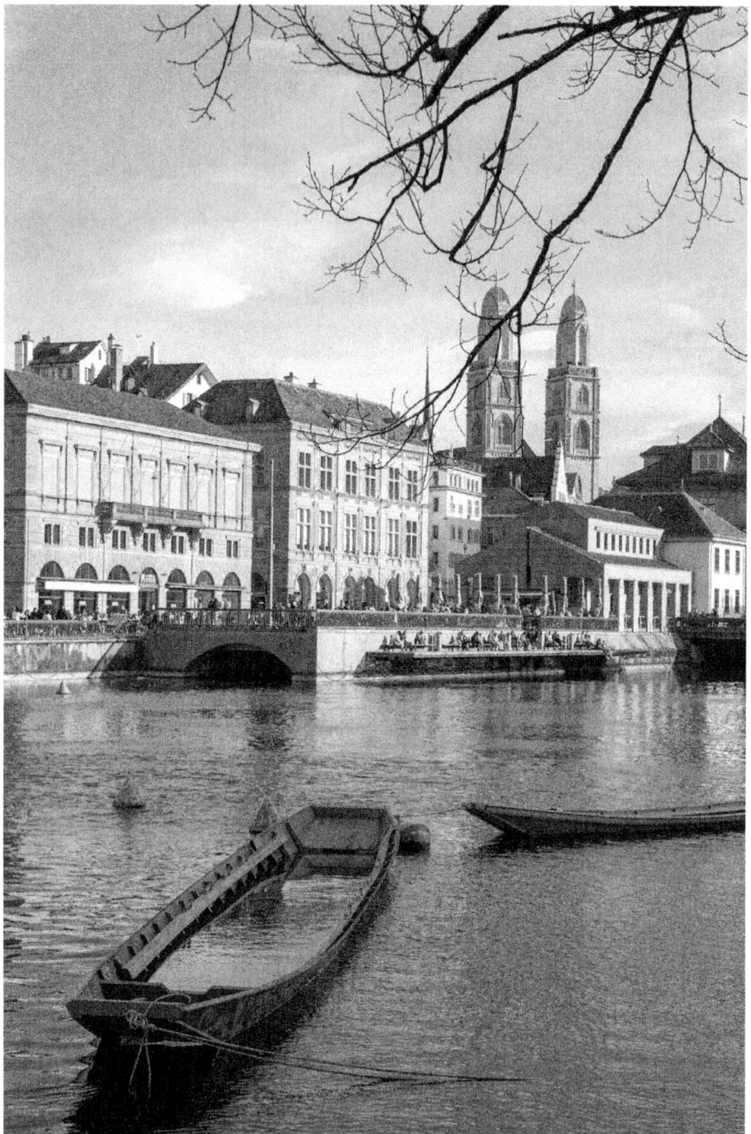

Chapter 6

Contemporary Culture and Creative Quirks

Welcome to Chapter 6, where we dive into the vibrant contemporary culture and creative quirks of Zurich. Get ready to explore the dynamic art scene, discover trendy neighborhoods and local hangouts, and embark on a journey through unique museums and eccentric exhibitions.

Explore Zurich's Vibrant Contemporary Art Scene

Are you ready to be inspired by the intersection of art and innovation? Zurich's contemporary art scene is a captivating blend of traditional techniques and boundary-pushing creativity. From world-renowned galleries to experimental art spaces, you'll find a treasure trove of artistic expression around every corner.

Kunsthaus Zurich: The Masterpieces

Start your artistic journey at the Kunsthaus Zurich, a cultural institution that houses an impressive collection of modern and contemporary art. Marvel at masterpieces by renowned artists like Picasso, Monet, and Chagall. As you explore the galleries, you'll witness the evolution of artistic styles and gain a deeper understanding of the creative forces that shape Zurich's art scene.

Let me help spike your imagination. Imagine you're strolling through the Kunsthaus Zurich, marveling at exquisite works of art by the great masters. You turn a corner and come face to face with a Picasso that takes your breath away.

But wait, what's that nearby? A piece of banana taped to the wall? Yep, that's right! It's an installation piece that sparked a whole banana drama in the art world. It's moments like these that make Zurich's contemporary art scene intriguing and full of surprises.

Löwenbräukunst and Schiffbau Art Complexes

If you're into cutting-edge contemporary art, head to the Löwenbräukunst and Schiffbau art complexes.

These innovative spaces showcase the works of both established and emerging artists, pushing the boundaries of artistic expression and challenging traditional norms. Immerse yourself in thought-provoking installations, multimedia exhibitions, and interactive displays that will ignite your imagination.

The Hipster's Haven: Trendy Neighborhoods and Local Hangouts

Welcome to the hipster's haven, where quirky vibes and coolness collide in the most extraordinary way. In this section, we'll explore Zurich's trendiest neighborhoods and local hangouts, where creativity thrives and unique experiences await. So, put on your beanie, grab your vintage camera, and let's dive into the hipster scene!

Kreis 4: Where Quirkiness Meets Coolness and Hipsters Roam Free

Imagine stepping into Kreis 4, a neighborhood bursting with creative energy and an unmistakable hipster flair.

This eclectic neighborhood is a melting pot of creativity, boasting an array of trendy cafes, vintage shops, and street art.

As you wander through its vibrant streets, you'll encounter colorful street art that tells stories of rebellion and self-expression. Stop by a cozy café where bearded baristas serve up artisanal coffee and grab a cup of artisanal coffee.

And if vintage is your thing, you'll find yourself lost in a treasure trove of vinyl records, retro fashion, and quirky accessories. Browse through vintage vinyl records, or simply soak up the vibrant atmosphere as you stroll along the colorful streets. Kreis 4 is a place where individuality is celebrated, and everyone's a trendsetter.

Zurich West: The Vibrant Viadukt

For a dose of alternative culture, head to Zurich West. Once an industrial area, this transformed district is now a hub of creativity and innovation. Explore the vibrant Viadukt, a renovated railway viaduct that houses trendy boutiques, design studios, and artisanal food markets.

Indulge in some retail therapy, sample local delicacies, and admire the striking architecture that blends old-world charm with modern aesthetics. Discover unique pieces of art, handmade crafts, and one-of-a-kind fashion finds.

Unique Museums and Eccentric Exhibitions: Prepare to be Mind-Blown!

Get ready to embark on a journey through curiosity as we step into Zurich's unique museums and eccentric exhibitions. In this section, we'll take a detour from the ordinary and venture into the realm of the peculiar and the extraordinary. Zurich's unique museums and eccentric exhibitions will tickle your imagination and leave you with unforgettable experiences.

Museum of Design: Quirky, Curious, and Unforgettable

Start your adventure at the Museum of Design, where you'll find a captivating blend of contemporary design, fashion, and applied arts.

From innovative furniture to avant-garde fashion, this museum celebrates the intersection of art and functionality. Be prepared to have your creative senses ignited and your perspectives challenged as you explore the ever-evolving world and immerse yourself in the realm of the curious and unconventional.

You might even stumble upon a chair that looks like a work of art but is actually a surprisingly comfortable seat. It's a place where practicality meets quirkiness and where you'll leave with a newfound appreciation for the blend of aesthetics and utility.

For a truly eccentric experience, don't miss out on the offbeat exhibitions that Zurich has to offer. These interactive and unexpected encounters will leave you both amused and bewildered, sparking conversations and opening up new perspectives on art and life.

During my own adventure through Zurich's eccentric exhibitions, I stumbled upon a talking sculpture that caught me completely off guard. As I approached the artwork, it suddenly started speaking, engaging me in a witty conversation that left me both amused and bewildered.

It was a surreal and comical experience that reminded me of the unexpected surprises that await in the world of quirky museums and eccentric exhibitions.

In the end, Zurich proves to be a haven for creativity, innovation, and unconventional experiences. So, go forth and embrace the vibrant energy of Zurich's contemporary culture.

How to Find Your Way to Zurich's Museums and Art Neighborhoods

The Tram: The tram system in Zurich is efficient and convenient, providing easy access to major art galleries and museums. Trams are affordable, and their extensive network covers most areas of the city.

Bus: Buses provide additional flexibility for reaching specific museums or exhibitions that may be located slightly off the tram routes. They offer convenient connections and ensure easy access to unique cultural experiences.

Bicycle: Zurich has a well-developed cycling infrastructure, making it a bike-friendly city. Renting a bicycle gives you the freedom to explore trendy neighborhoods like Kreis 4 and Zurich West at your own pace.

Walking: Zurich's art scene is concentrated in the city center, making it easily accessible on foot. Walking allows you to soak in the city's ambiance, stumble upon hidden gems, and discover street art and installations in unexpected places.

My Recommendation

For visiting art galleries and museums, I recommend a combination of walking and taking the tram. Walking allows you to explore at your own pace and stumble upon unexpected art installations, while the tram provides efficient transportation between different art destinations.

If you're up for some adventure, renting a bicycle is a fantastic option to explore Zurich's hipster neighborhoods. It allows you to blend in with the local culture, experience the city like a true Zurich resident, and embrace the trendy atmosphere at your own leisure.

Chapter 7

Retail Therapy: Shopping Extravaganza

Welcome to another exciting side of Zurich, where we indulge in the exhilarating world of retail therapy. Get ready to explore the city's fashion-forward shopping districts, unearth retro treasures in flea markets and thrift stores, and discover locally crafted Swiss souvenirs to bring home.

Whether you're a fashionista, a vintage enthusiast, or simply on the hunt for unique keepsakes, Zurich offers a shopping extravaganza that will leave you wanting more. So, grab your shopping bags, and let's dive into this retail adventure together!

Boutique Bliss: Fashion Forward Shopping Districts

Prepare to be dazzled by Zurich's fashion-forward shopping districts, where boutique bliss awaits.

From luxury brands to independent designers, these districts cater to every fashion taste and style.

Bahnhofstrasse: Where Fashion Dreams Come True (And So Does Your Credit Card Balance)

Head to Bahnhofstrasse, Zurich's most famous shopping street and a paradise for high-end fashion enthusiasts. Marvel at the stunning window displays of prestigious international brands and step into luxurious boutiques that showcase the latest trends in fashion and accessories. Whether you're looking for a statement piece or an elegant ensemble, Bahnhofstrasse will satisfy your sartorial desires.

Niederdorf and Kreis 5: Because Shopping is Cheaper Than a Psychiatrist!

For a more eclectic and alternative shopping experience, venture into Zurich's trendy neighborhoods like Niederdorf and Kreis 5.

These vibrant areas are dotted with independent boutiques, concept stores, and local designer studios. Explore hidden gems and discover unique, fashion-forward pieces that reflect Zurich's vibrant and diverse fashion scene.

Vintage Vista: Discover Retro Treasures in Flea Markets and Thrift Stores

If you're a fan of all things vintage, Zurich has a treat in store for you. Embark on a journey to unearth retro treasures in flea markets and thrift stores that hold stories from the past.

Kanzlei Flea Market: Time Travel Through Fashion (And Find Your Inner Hipster)

Visit the popular Kanzlei Flea Market, where you can rummage through a diverse selection of second-hand items, from vintage clothing and accessories to vinyl records, second-hand items, and antique collectibles. Embrace the thrill of the hunt as you browse through stalls, discovering hidden gems and one-of-a-kind pieces that will add a touch of nostalgia to your wardrobe or home.

Vintage Boutiques and Consignment Stores

For a curated vintage experience, explore Zurich's vintage boutiques and consignment stores. These carefully curated spaces offer a wide array of retro clothing, accessories, and home decor items. Let the nostalgia wash over you as you step back in time and find unique pieces that reflect your individual style.

Swiss Souvenirs: Locally Crafted Keepsakes to Bring Home

No visit to Zurich is complete without taking home some Swiss souvenirs. Explore the local craft scene and discover keepsakes that capture the essence of Switzerland's rich cultural heritage.

Old Town Picks: From Swiss Army Knives to Chocolate Delights

Because who doesn't need a pocket knife and Some Sweet Indulgence? Head to the charming Old Town, where you'll find traditional Swiss souvenir shops selling exquisite, handcrafted items. From intricate Swiss watches to delicate Swiss chocolates, these shops offer a range of souvenirs that represent the country's craftsmanship and attention to detail.

No matter which shopping experience you choose, it's important to keep in mind that prices can vary depending on the items you're looking for. Luxury boutiques and high-end stores in Bahnhofstrasse may come with a higher price tag, while flea markets and thrift stores offer more budget-friendly options.

How to Move Around While Shopping in Zurich

To make your shopping adventure in Zurich a breeze, let's discuss the available transport modes and the best ways to reach the various shopping destinations we talked about.

Walking: When it comes to transportation for your shopping extravaganza, walking is often the best way to navigate Zurich's shopping districts. Many of these areas are pedestrian-friendly, allowing you to leisurely explore the shops and soak in the vibrant atmosphere. Plus, walking gives you the opportunity to stumble upon hidden gems and local discoveries along the way.

Bahnhofstrasse shopping street is conveniently located in the heart of Zurich, making it easily accessible on foot from many central locations.

Vintage Boutiques and Consignment Stores are often scattered throughout different neighborhoods in Zurich. Walking is a fantastic way to discover these stores, as it allows you to stumble upon unexpected vintage delights tucked away in charming corners.

Also, if you're exploring Zurich's Old Town, walking is the ideal mode of transport. Not only will you enjoy the picturesque streets and historic buildings, but you'll also have the freedom to pop in and out of various shops as you please. Plus, the close proximity of the shops within the Old Town makes it convenient to navigate on foot.

Trams and Buses: If you prefer public transportation, trams and buses are available to connect you to different parts of the city. Also, if you're staying a bit further away from Bahnhofstrasse, Zurich's efficient tram and bus network can transport you to this fashionable district.

Trams and buses are a cost-effective and time-efficient way to reach your destination while enjoying the city sights along the way. Just check the public transport schedules, hop on board, purchase a ticket, and you're on your way to retail bliss.

Ultimately, the best mode of transport depends on your location and personal preferences. Consider the distances, check the local transport schedules, and choose the mode of transport that best suits your shopping itinerary. Happy shopping and exploring!

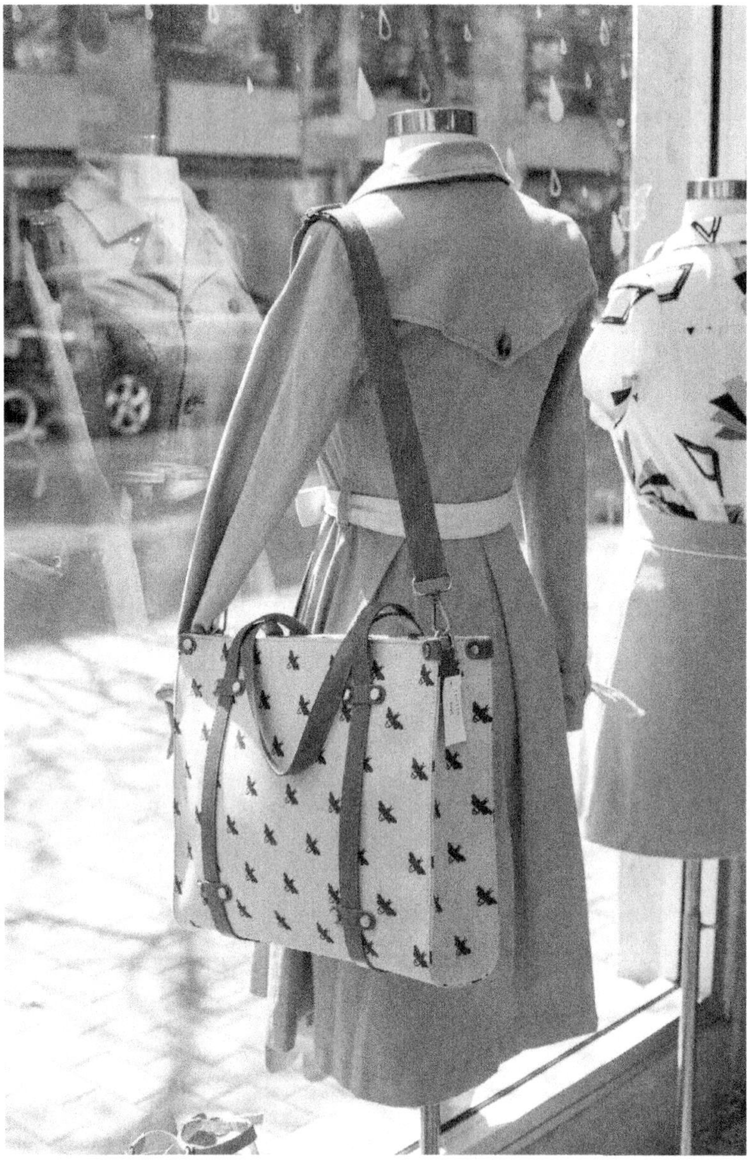

Chapter 8

Adventure Awaits: Day Trips from Zurich

Get ready for some thrilling day trips from Zurich as we embark on unforgettable adventures. From alpine escapades to exploring medieval marvels and indulging in Swiss vintages, there's something for every adventure seeker.

Alpine Escapades: Skiing, Hiking, and Nature's Marvels

Calling all nature enthusiasts and adrenaline junkies! In this section, we'll explore the alpine wonders surrounding Zurich, where thrilling outdoor activities and breathtaking landscapes await.

Hit the slopes and experience world-class skiing and snowboarding in the Swiss Alps. From the iconic resorts of Zermatt and St. Moritz to the lesser-known gems like Flumserberg and Engelberg, the options are endless.

Glide down powdery slopes, soak in mesmerizing mountain vistas, and indulge in après-ski delights that will warm your heart and soul.

When the snow melts, the Swiss Alps transform into a hiker's paradise. Lace up your hiking boots and embark on scenic trails that lead to majestic peaks, crystal-clear lakes, and picturesque valleys.

Explore the Jungfrau region, hike the trails of Ebenalp and Santis, or take a stroll around the idyllic Lake Lucerne. The alpine beauty will leave you in awe, and the fresh mountain air will rejuvenate your spirit.

Castles and Countryside: Medieval Marvels Beyond the City

Prepare to step back in time as we venture beyond Zurich to discover captivating castles and charming countryside landscapes. Delve into Switzerland's rich history and immerse yourself in the medieval wonders that await.

Castle Quest: The Chillon Castle

Visit the majestic Chillon Castle on the shores of Lake Geneva, known for its fairytale-like appearance and intriguing history. Explore the well-preserved halls, secret passages, and stunning lake views, and feel like you've stepped into a medieval tale.

Scenic Villages: Stein, Rhein and Murten

Take a leisurely drive through the countryside and discover quaint Swiss villages like Stein am Rhein and Murten. Wander through cobblestone streets lined with half-timbered houses, explore local shops and cafes, and soak up the tranquil ambiance of these hidden gems.

Wine Tasting and Vineyard Hopping: Discover Swiss Vintages

Indulge in the rich flavors and aromas of Swiss wines as we explore the vineyards and wineries surrounding Zurich.

Switzerland's wine regions are a delight for wine enthusiasts and offer a unique blend of traditional winemaking and stunning landscapes.

Wine Wonderland: The Lavaux Region

Journey to the picturesque region of Lavaux, a UNESCO World Heritage site renowned for its terraced vineyards. Take a leisurely stroll along the vineyard trails, sample exquisite wines at local wineries, and savor the breathtaking views of Lake Geneva and the Alps.

Zurich's Wine Route: Swiss' Most Exotic Vineyards

Closer to the city, the Zurich Wine Route offers a delightful wine-tasting experience. Visit vineyards in the nearby towns of Winterthur, Meilen, and Dielsdorf, and discover the diverse range of Swiss varietals produced in the region. From crisp whites to velvety reds, you'll have the opportunity to taste and learn about Swiss wines straight from the source.

How to Find Your Way Around

The Skiing and Snowboarding Resorts: The most convenient way to reach the ski resorts is by train. Switzerland's well-connected rail network will take you directly to popular skiing destinations like Zermatt, St. Moritz, Flumserberg, and Engelberg. Train tickets are generally affordable, and the journey itself offers scenic views of the Swiss countryside. Once you arrive, resort shuttles or cable cars can transport you to the slopes.

The Hiking Trails and Mountain Areas: For hiking adventures in the Swiss Alps, trains are also the preferred mode of transport. They provide access to various starting points, such as Interlaken for the Jungfrau region or Appenzell for Ebenalp and Santis. Trains offer a comfortable and efficient way to reach these areas, and you can enjoy the breathtaking scenery along the way.

Chillon Castle: To reach Chillon Castle, located near Montreux on Lake Geneva, you can take a direct train from Zurich to Montreux.

The train ride takes around two hours and offers picturesque views along Lake Geneva. From Montreux, the castle is within walking distance or a short bus ride away.

Scenic Villages: Exploring the scenic Swiss countryside and visiting villages like Stein am Rhein and Murten is best done by a combination of train and regional buses. Trains from Zurich will take you to the respective towns, and from there, local buses can transport you to specific villages. The schedules are well-coordinated, and buses are equipped to accommodate visitors.

Lavaux Region: To reach the Lavaux vineyards near Lake Geneva, you can take a train from Zurich to Lausanne or Vevey. From there, local trains or buses will take you to various points within the Lavaux region. Alternatively, you can also take a boat ride on Lake Geneva, which allows you to admire the picturesque vineyards from the water.

Zurich Wine Route: Exploring the local wine scene around Zurich can be done using a combination of public transport options.

Trains and regional buses connect Zurich with towns like Winterthur, Meilen, and Dielsdorf, where you can visit vineyards and wineries. Local transportation within these towns is easily accessible, ensuring a smooth wine-tasting experience.

Best Means of Transport for Day Trips

Public Transportation: Switzerland's efficient and well-connected public transport system is often the most convenient and cost-effective way to reach day trip destinations. Trains, buses, and boats are readily available, offering scenic routes and reliable schedules. Check the local transport websites for information on routes, timetables, and ticket prices.

Car Rental: If you prefer the flexibility of exploring at your own pace, renting a car can be a great option. It allows you to venture off the beaten path, stop at scenic viewpoints, and visit multiple destinations in a single day. Keep in mind that parking availability and costs may vary, especially in popular tourist areas.

Guided Tours: Another great option is to join a guided tour specifically tailored to the day trip you're interested in. These tours often provide transportation, knowledgeable guides, and a structured itinerary, making it a hassle-free option for those who prefer a more organized experience.

PS. In terms of cost, train tickets in Switzerland can be relatively expensive compared to buses. However, trains offer a faster and more comfortable travel experience. Regional buses and boats are generally more affordable, but they may have longer travel times.

Ultimately, the best mode of transport depends on your preferences, budget, and the specific day trip you plan to take. Consider factors like travel time, distance, accessibility of the transport mode, your budget convenience, and the overall experience you desire.

Remember to check transportation schedules in advance, especially for public transport, to ensure you have enough time to explore and return to Zurich comfortably.

Chapter 9

From Festivals to Fond Farewells: Experiencing Zurich's Events

Welcome to Chapter 9, where we dive into the vibrant festival scene of Zurich. Get ready to immerse yourself in a world of revelry, music, and celebration. From carnival capers to summer fiestas and sparkling New Year's Eve spectacles, Zurich knows how to throw a party. Get ready to immerse yourself in the joyous atmosphere and create memories that will last a lifetime!

Carnival Capers: Revelry, Masks, and Merriment

When it comes to carnivals, Zurich knows how to let loose and have a good time. The city comes alive with colorful parades, lively music, and a contagious festive spirit.

Join the locals and visitors as they don their elaborate costumes and masks, transforming the streets into a vibrant tapestry of colors. From traditional processions to street parties, carnival in Zurich is a time to celebrate and embrace the joy of life.

Zurich Carnival: Let the Good Times Roll

The main carnival event in Zurich is the "Zurich Carnival," also known as "Fasnacht." This annual extravaganza takes place in late winter or early spring and features parades, music, and street performances.

Marvel at the intricately designed floats, dance to the lively tunes of the Guggenmusik bands and indulge in traditional carnival treats like "Fasnachtskiechli" (deep-fried pastries).

The vibrant Atmosphere is one you do not want to miss. Experience the contagious energy and joy that fills the air during the carnival festivities. It is also a perfect time to immerse yourself in Swiss traditions and witness the unique customs associated with the carnival.

Summer Fiestas and Music Melodies: Embracing Zurich's Festive Spirit

When summer arrives, Zurich transforms into a hub of outdoor festivities and music-filled evenings. The city embraces a multitude of open-air concerts, festivals, and cultural events, offering a delightful blend of local and international talents.

Zurich Street Parade: Unleash Your Inner Party Animal

One of the most anticipated summer events is the "Zurich Street Parade," a vibrant electronic music festival that takes over the streets of Zurich. Join thousands of party-goers as they dance to the beats of renowned DJs, admire colorful parade floats, and soak up the lively atmosphere.

Let your worries melt away as you groove to the rhythm of the city. You also get to enjoy the pleasant summer weather as you participate in open-air concerts and street celebrations.

Countdown to Fun: New Year's Eve in Zurich

As the year comes to a close, Zurich transforms into a sparkling wonderland for its New Year's Eve celebrations. Join the festive crowds as they gather around the iconic landmarks, eagerly awaiting the stroke of midnight. Prepare to be dazzled by stunning fireworks displays, festive markets, and a joyful atmosphere that fills the streets.

Head to the iconic Zurich Lake to witness the spectacular New Year's Eve fireworks, illuminating the night sky in a dazzling array of colors. Join the crowds in Bahnhofstrasse, where you can browse through the enchanting Christmas markets, sip on mulled wine, and indulge in delectable treats.

Movie Magic: Behind the Scenes at Zurich's Film Festival

While Zurich is known for its vibrant events throughout the year, there are a few more festivals that visitors should not miss. One is the Zurich Film Festival. For movie enthusiasts, the Zurich Film Festival is a must-attend event.

Held annually in September, this festival showcases a diverse selection of international and Swiss films, ranging from feature films to documentaries. Enjoy screenings, Q&A sessions with filmmakers, and red-carpet events, all while soaking up the glamour of the silver screen.

Sechseläuten: Böögg Burning and Springtime Revelry

Sechseläuten is an iconic spring festival in Zurich celebrated on the third Monday in April. The highlight of the festival is the traditional "Böögg" burning, where a snowman-like figure representing winter is set on fire. The time it takes for the Böögg's head to explode is believed to predict the coming summer's weather. Join the locals as they cheer and celebrate the arrival of warmer days.

Food, Wine, and Everything Divine: Gastronomic Festivals in Zurich

Food lovers should not miss Zurich's Street Food Festival, held multiple times throughout the year.

This culinary extravaganza brings together a wide variety of international cuisines, from mouthwatering street food delicacies to gourmet delights. Explore the diverse food stalls, savor the flavors from around the world, and enjoy the lively atmosphere with live music and entertainment.

Christmas Markets

Zurich's Christmas markets are a beloved tradition that should not be missed during the holiday season. The most popular markets are located in the city center at Bahnhofstrasse, Zurich Main Station, and Bellevueplatz. Immerse yourself in the enchanting atmosphere, browse through the festive stalls selling crafts and treats, and sip on mulled wine as you embrace the magic of the holiday season.

These are just a few examples of the many exciting festivals that take place in Zurich throughout the year. Keep an eye on the local event calendars and tourist information for the most up-to-date information on upcoming festivals and events during your visit.

Chapter 10

Insider Tips: Making the Most of Your Zurich Adventure

Welcome to the final chapter, where I unveil insider tips to help you make the most of your Zurich adventure. From language and cultural etiquette to weather considerations and money matters, these insights will ensure a smooth and enjoyable experience as you navigate through the Swiss way of life. So, let's dive in and uncover the secrets to becoming a savvy Zurich explorer!

Language and Cultural Etiquette: Embrace the Swiss Way of Life

Language: While Zurich is predominantly German-speaking, English is widely spoken, especially in tourist areas. However, learning a few basic German phrases can go a long way in interacting with locals and immersing yourself in Swiss culture.

So, don't be shy to greet with a friendly "Guten Tag" or say "Danke" (thank you) when receiving excellent service.

Cultural Etiquette: Switzerland prides itself on its punctuality and respect for personal space. Arriving on time for appointments and being mindful of queueing etiquette are valued cultural norms. When you're not sure how to act in a situation, observe the locals and take the hint. Remember, a smile and a polite demeanor will always go a long way in forging connections and creating memorable experiences.

Weather Wonders: Dress for the Seasons and Climate

Zurich experiences distinct seasons, each with its own charm and weather considerations. Here's a breakdown of what to expect and how to dress accordingly:

Spring: Spring in Zurich brings mild temperatures, blooming flowers, and occasional rain showers.

Layering is key during this season, as temperatures can vary throughout the day. Pack a lightweight jacket or sweater, comfortable walking shoes, and an umbrella to stay prepared for any weather surprises.

Summer: Summers in Zurich are pleasant, with warm temperatures and longer daylight hours. Dress in lightweight and breathable clothing, such as cotton shirts, shorts, and comfortable walking shoes. Don't forget to bring sunscreen, a hat, and sunglasses to protect yourself from the sun while exploring the city's outdoor attractions.

Autumn: Autumn showcases Zurich's picturesque colors as the leaves change to vibrant hues. The temperatures start to cool, so it's advisable to pack layers, including a light jacket or sweater. Comfortable walking shoes are still essential for exploring the city's parks and gardens.

Winter: Winter in Zurich brings chilly temperatures and occasional snowfall, transforming the city into a winter wonderland.

Bundle up with warm coats, scarves, gloves, and hats to stay cozy while exploring the Christmas markets or enjoying winter sports. Don't forget to wear sturdy, waterproof boots for walking on snowy or icy surfaces.

Money Matters: Currency, Tipping, and Budgeting Advice

Currency: The official currency in Zurich is the Swiss Franc (CHF). While credit cards are widely accepted, it's advisable to carry some cash for small establishments or when visiting markets. Currency exchange services are available at airports, train stations, and banks throughout the city.

Tipping: Tipping in Zurich is not mandatory, as service charges are usually included in the bill. However, it is common to round up the bill or leave a small tip for excellent service. If you receive exceptional service, feel free to show your appreciation with a more generous tip.

Budgeting: Zurich is known for its high standard of living, and it's important to plan your budget accordingly. While some attractions and activities may have entry fees, there are also plenty of free or low-cost options to explore, such as parks, public gardens, and walking tours.

Consider purchasing the Zurich Card, which provides unlimited access to public transportation and discounts on various attractions, making it a cost-effective option for exploring the city.

Ultimately, by incorporating these insider tips into your Zurich adventure, you'll enhance your overall experience and make lasting memories. So, get ready to immerse yourself in the Swiss culture, explore with confidence, and create unforgettable moments in this vibrant city!

94 | The Complete Zurich Travel Guide 2023

Conclusion

Forever Enamored: Leaving Zurich with Memories That Last

As we come to the end of our journey through Zurich, it's time to reflect on the incredible experiences, hidden gems, and unforgettable moments that have made this city so special.

Throughout our exploration, we've unveiled the secrets of the Altstadt and ventured into surprising side streets, unearthing unexpected treasures off the beaten path. We've relaxed by the serene shores of Lake Zurich, cruised its crystal waters, and embraced the wonders of nature.

We've experienced the thrill of alpine escapades, explored majestic mountains, castles, and vineyards. We've embarked on shopping extravaganzas and unearthed retro treasures in flea markets and thrift stores. We've also immersed ourselves in the festive spirit of Zurich.

And throughout our journey, we've navigated the city's transportation systems, from flights and trains to trams, boats, and bicycles. But as our time in Zurich comes to a close, we must bid farewell to this enchanting city.

However, the memories we've created will forever be etched in our hearts. Zurich has not only been a destination but a source of inspiration and a place where adventures have come alive.

So, as you reluctantly pack your bags and prepare to leave, remember that your journey doesn't end here. The spirit of this vibrant city will continue to inspire us, reminding us of the beauty of exploration, the joy of discovery, and the magic of travel.

Thank you for joining me on this exhilarating adventure through Zurich. I hope this travel guide has provided you with valuable insights, helpful tips, and a glimpse into the wonders of this remarkable city.

May your future travels be filled with excitement, laughter, and captivating destinations. Farewell, dear reader, until we meet again on another grand adventure!

Bon Voyage! Maps and Helpful Resources for Your Zurich Adventure

As you prepare to embark on your Zurich adventure, I'll want to equip you with some practical tips, useful maps, and helpful resources to ensure a smooth and enjoyable journey.

Whether you're a first-time visitor or a seasoned traveler, having the right information at your fingertips can make all the difference in making the most of your Zurich experience. So, dive in and arm yourself with the tools you need for a memorable trip!

Maps and Navigation

Zurich City Map: Familiarize yourself with the layout of the city by obtaining a detailed map, available at tourist information centers or through online resources. This will help you navigate the streets, locate attractions, and plan your itinerary efficiently.

Public Transportation Map: Zurich has an excellent public transportation system consisting of trams, buses, and trains. Acquire a public transportation map to easily navigate the city and make use of the extensive network.

Mobile Apps: Consider downloading mobile apps like "SBB Mobile" for train schedules and tickets, "Zurich Public Transport" for tram and bus information, and "Google Maps" for general navigation assistance.

Helpful Resources

Tourist Information Centers: Zurich has several tourist information centers throughout the city, where friendly staff can provide you with maps, brochures, and insider tips. They can also assist you in booking tours, acquiring city cards, or answering any queries you may have.

Official Websites: Visit the official Zurich tourism website and other reputable travel websites for information on attractions, events, accommodations, and more.

One important website is the Zurich Card website: https://www.zuerich.com/en.

These websites often provide valuable insights, special offers, and updates on city happenings.

Local Recommendations: Don't hesitate to ask locals or seek recommendations from hotel staff, restaurant owners, or fellow travelers. Locals can provide insider tips, hidden gems, and off-the-beaten-path experiences that might not be mentioned in guidebooks.

Armed with these practical tips, maps, and helpful resources, you're now ready to embark on your Zurich adventure.

Note: Please ensure to check the latest travel advisories and guidelines before your trip, as situations and regulations may change. Remember to stay curious, embrace the local culture, and savor every moment of this enchanting city.

Bon voyage, and enjoy your unforgettable journey through Zurich!

Printed in Great Britain
by Amazon